1.3

Read Together

Hello, Reader!

Each day you are becoming a better reader. Good for you!

The stories in this book will take you to the ocean and to neighborhood streets. You will visit a watermelon patch and a rain forest. Can you guess who lives in each of these places? Read to find out.

You may even find some Surprises along the way.

HOUGHTON MIFFLIN

Reading

Surprises

Senior Authors
J. David Cooper
John J. Pikulski

Authors
Patricia A. Ackerman
Kathryn H. Au
David J. Chard
Gilbert G. Garcia
Claude N. Goldenberg
Marjorie Y. Lipson
Susan E. Page
Shane Templeton
Sheila W. Valencia
MaryEllen Vogt

Consultants
Linda H. Butler
Linnea C. Ehri
Carla B. Ford

HOUGHTON MIFFLIN
Reading
A Legacy of Literacy

HOUGHTON MIFFLIN   BOSTON • MORRIS PLAINS, NJ

California • Colorado • Georgia • Illinois • New Jersey • Texas

Cover and title page photography by Tony Scarpetta.

Cover photography © Nic Bishop Photography.

Acknowledgments begin on page 232.

ISBN: 0-618-25779-9

3 4 5 6 7 8 9 10 DW 11 10 09 08 07 06 05 04 03 02

Home Sweet Home 12

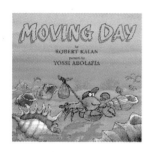

Phonics Library:
Pets in a Tank
Gram's Trip
Stuck in the House

Pets in a Tank
by Gary Demas
illustrated by Eduardo Espada

Kate and Jake spot a big
tank. Kate and Jake think
they will get a pet.

realistic
fiction

Phonics Library:
Pine Lake
Fun Rides
Jim and Sal

Big Book

Winter Lullaby
*by Barbara Seuling
illustrated by Greg
Newbold*

On My Way Practice Readers

The Chip Chop Ship
by Morgan Henry

**What Can You See at
a Lake?**
by Mindy Menschell

**Stripe and the Nice
Mice**
by Nicolas Thilo-McGovern

Theme Paperbacks

Greetings, Sun
*by Phillis and
David Gershator
illustrated by
Synthia St. James*

🎗 Americas Award
Commended List

The Leaving Morning
*by Angela Johnson
illustrated by
David Soman*

🎗 Bank Street College
Best Children's Books
of the Year
CCBC "Choices"

 Technology

Visit www.eduplace.com/kids **Education Place**®

Read at school Accelerated Reader®

Read at home www.bookadventure.org

Focus on

Poetry

Animal Adventures 128

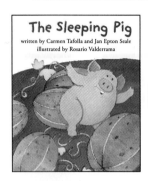

fantasy

Student Writing Model

Phonics Library:
Duke's Gift
Legs Gets His Lunch
The Nest

Phonics Library:
Seal Beach
Pete and Peach
Gram's Huge Meal

9

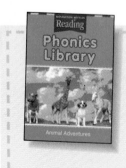

Phonics Library:
Rain Day
Cub's Long Day
Jay's Trip

Additional Resources

Big Book

Two's Company
by Shirley Greenway

On My Way Practice Readers

Fox and Mule
by Lin Kwok

What Animal Is It?
by Oscar Gake

The Real Wolf
by Nicolas Grant

Theme Paperbacks

The Little Red Hen
by Harriet Ziefert
illustrated by
Emily Bolam

Fishing Bears
by Ruth Berman
photographs by
Lynn M. Stone

Technology

Visit **www.eduplace.com/kids** *Education Place*®

Read at school **Accelerated Reader**™

Read at home **www.bookadventure.org** *Book Adventure*™

11

Home Sweet Home

The Very Nicest Place

The fish lives in the brook,
The bird lives in the tree,
But home's the very
    nicest place
For a little child like me.

Anonymous

14

A Home in a Shell

The next story you will read is about a crab who has grown too big for its shell. Will the crab find a new home?

Words to Know

grow	room
light	these
long	this
more	that's
other	smooth
right	why
small	

Practice Sentences

1. There is no more room to grow in this shell.

2. That's why I must find a new shell.

3. This one is too long.

4. This one is too light.

5. This one is too smooth.

6. These other small shells are not right!

7. This shell is the best match.

MOVING DAY

by
ROBERT KALAN

pictures by
YOSSI ABOLAFIA

Strategy Focus

Read Together

As you read the story, ask yourself about the kinds of shells the hermit crab finds.

16

This shell is snug.

This shell is tight.

I will find a shell that's right.

This shell is too big.

This shell is too small.

Too big, too small,
these shells will not do at all.

21

This shell is too long.

This shell is too wide.

Too long, too wide,
too big, too small,
these shells will not do at all.

25

This shell is too heavy.

This shell is too light.

Too heavy, too light,
too long, too wide,
too big, too small,
these shells will not do at all.

29

This shell is too rough.

This shell is too smooth.

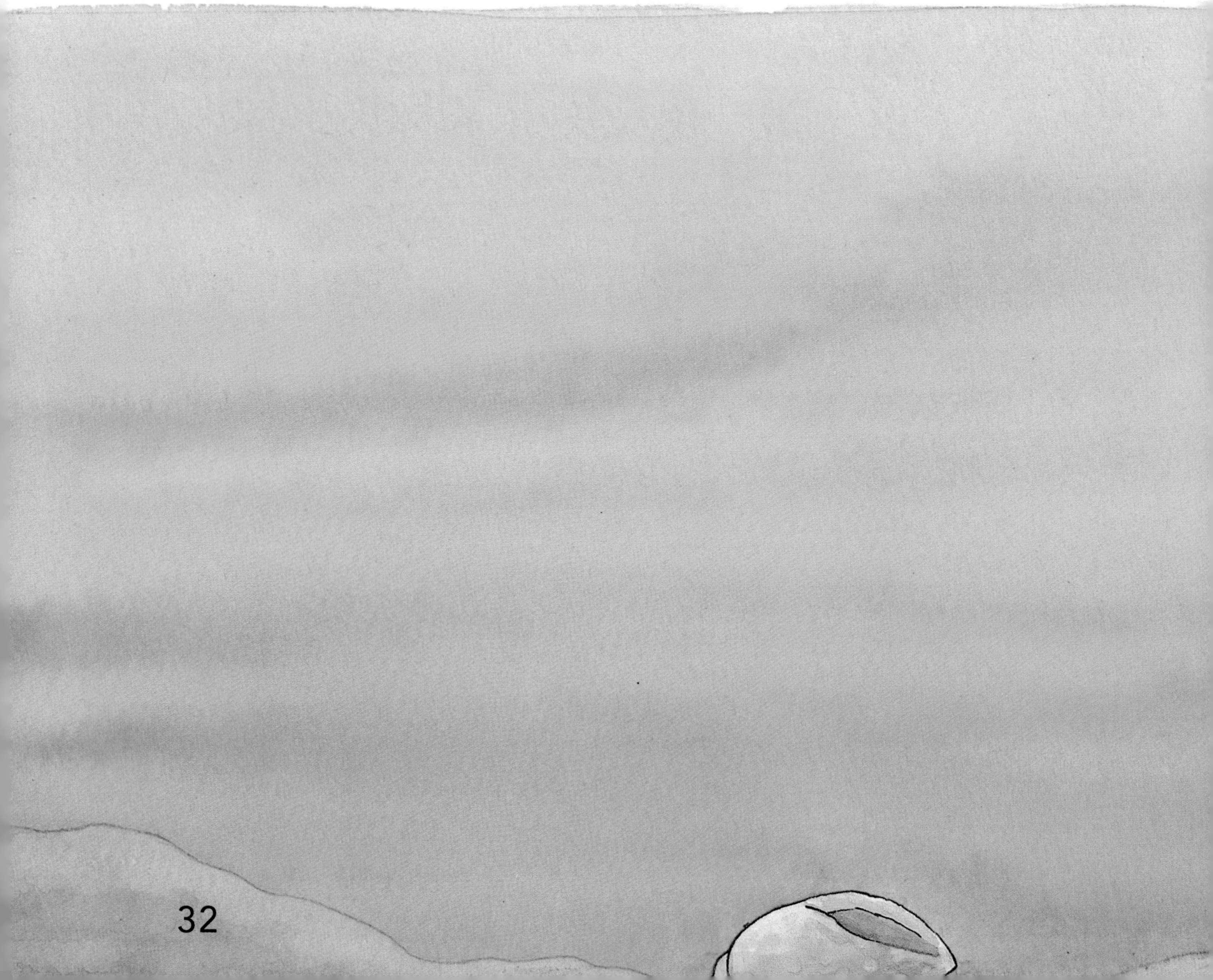

Too rough, too smooth,
too heavy, too light,
too long, too wide,
too big, too small,
these shells will not do at all.

This shell is too fancy.

This shell is too plain.

Too fancy,

 too plain,

too rough,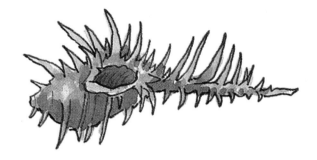

 too smooth,

too heavy,

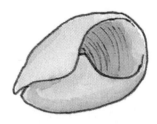 too light,

too long,

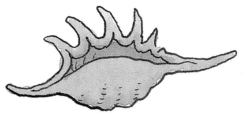 too wide,

too big,

 too small,

these shells will
not do at all.

This shell is too —

Wait!

It's NOT too snug.
It's NOT too tight.
This shell is the one that's right.

This shell has more room inside.
Room to grow, room to hide.

I know why this shell is fine.
It's like that other shell of mine.

Meet the Author and the Illustrator

Robert Kalan knows a lot about reading. He was once a kindergarten teacher. Today he likes writing animal stories.

Yossi Abolafia drew cartoons for TV. Now he draws comic strips for newspapers. He tries to tell stories with his pictures.

Internet

To find out more about Robert Kalan and Yossi Abolafia, visit Education Place.

www.eduplace.com/kids

43

Responding

Think About the Story

1. Why did it take a long time for the hermit crab to find the right home?

2. What did the crab learn about shells?

3. When will the crab need to find a new home?

Internet

Go on a Web Field Trip

Learn more about crabs and other animals that live at the seashore. Visit Education Place.

www.eduplace.com/kids

Compare Pictures

Look carefully at the color, shape, and size of each shell in the story. Describe to a partner what each shell looks like.

Informing

Write the Answer to a Question

What did the hermit crab learn by the end of the story? Write a sentence to answer the question.

Tips

- Start your sentence with a capital letter.
- End your sentence with a period.

Hermit Crabs

What's it like to pull your house on your back? Ask a hermit crab – it would know!

Many crabs have a hard shell, but not the hermit crab. Its back is soft.

The hermit must look for a shell that does not have an animal in it. The hermit gets in the shell and pulls it along.

If an animal comes, the crab ducks in the shell and hides.

47

This hermit is much too big for its shell. It must switch shells. Here's a big shell! The hermit pulls out of its first house. Then it pops right in the new one.

If you go to the seashore, look for a shell that walks. Is a hermit in it? What a crab!

49

A Personal Narrative

A personal narrative is a true story about something that happened to the writer. Use this student's writing as a model when you write a personal narrative of your own.

> A good **beginning** tells what the narrative is about.

> **Details** help the reader picture what happened.

The Lost Turtle

I lost my turtle. His name is Herman. I put up signs all around Jacksonville. So every day I sat by the phone. It was not fun when he was gone.

I cried and cried. And then when I was walking I saw Herman. We had a party. I was glad he was back.

A good **ending** wraps up the narrative.

Herman

Meet the Author

Hanna N.

Grade: one

State: Florida

Hobbies: drawing and reading

What she'd like to be when she grows up: a daycare teacher

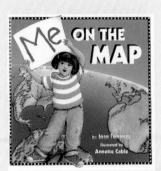

Where in the World?

In the next story, you will read about a girl who finds her place on the map. Watch for all the maps she draws!

Words to Know

could	think
house	world
how	state
over	place
own	find
so	

Practice Sentences

1. The world is a big place.
2. Do you think you could find your place on a map?
3. Here's how I do it.
4. I start with my own house and my street.
5. Then I find my town, my state, and my country.
6. So look over a map and find your place on it.

Meet the Author and the Illustrator

When she was little, **Joan Sweeney** liked art classes. Later she worked at a newspaper. This is her first book.

Annette Cable's pictures show us what our world looks like. She uses maps to show different places. Her drawings make learning about maps fun.

Internet

You can find out more about Joan Sweeney and Annette Cable at Education Place.

www.eduplace.com/kids

54

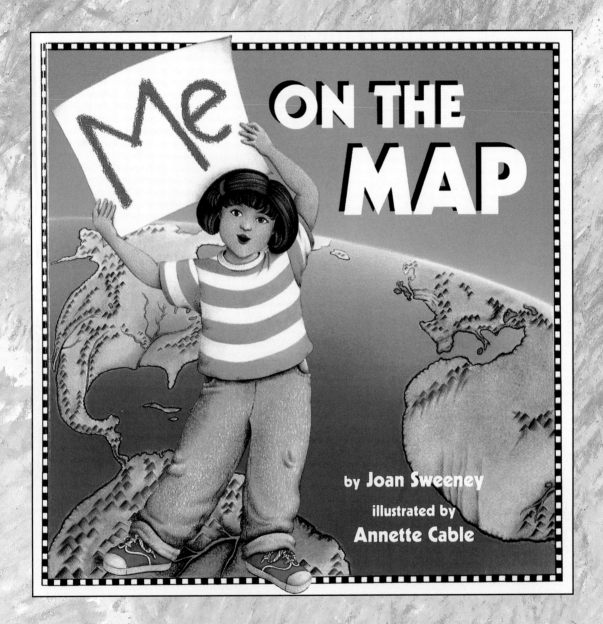

Me ON THE MAP

by Joan Sweeney

illustrated by Annette Cable

Strategy Focus

Read Together   Stop partway through the story and think about some of the places you have seen.

This is me.

This is me in my room.

56

This is a map of my room.

This is me on the map of my room.

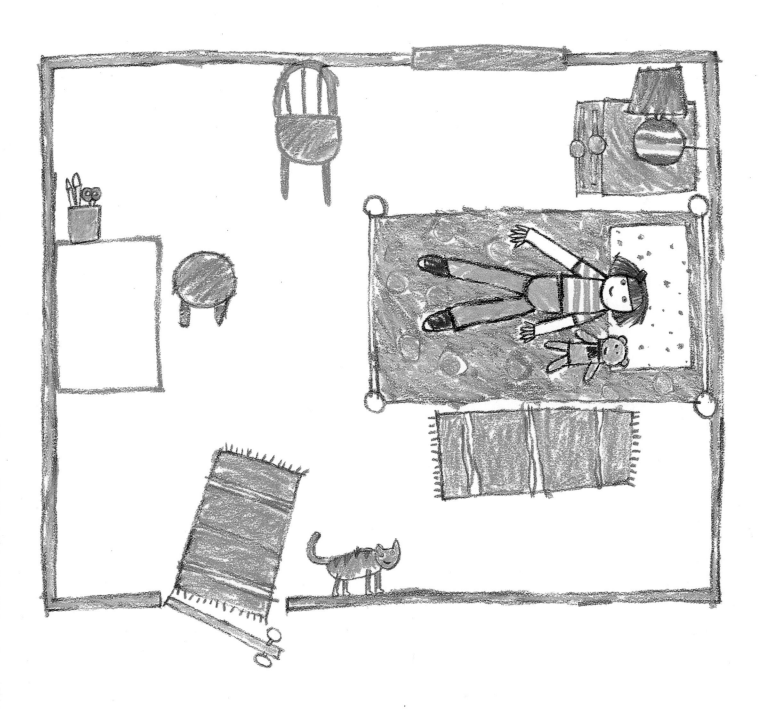

This is my house.

This is a map of my house.

This is my room on the map of my house.

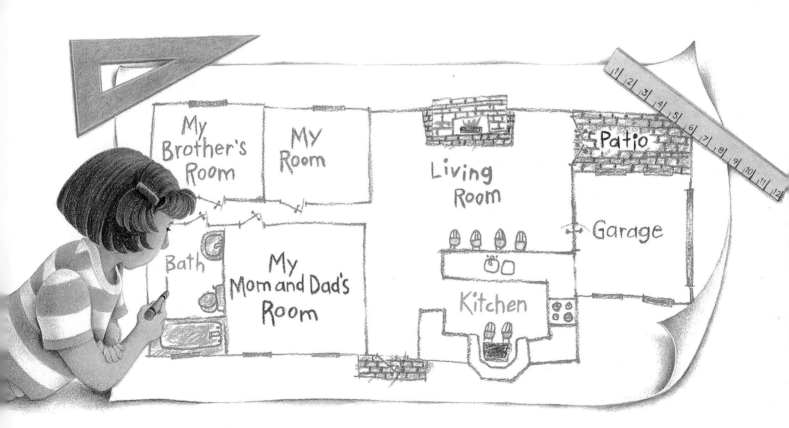

This is my street.

This is a map of my street.

This is my house on the map of my street.

This is my town.

This is a map of my town.

This is my street on the map of my town.

This is my state.

This is a map of my state.
This is my town on the map of my state.

This is my country.
The United States of America.

This is a map of my country.

This is my state on the map of my country.

This is my world. It is called Earth.
It looks like a giant ball.

If you could unroll the world and make it flat . . .

. . . it would look something like this map of the world.

This is my country on the map of the world.

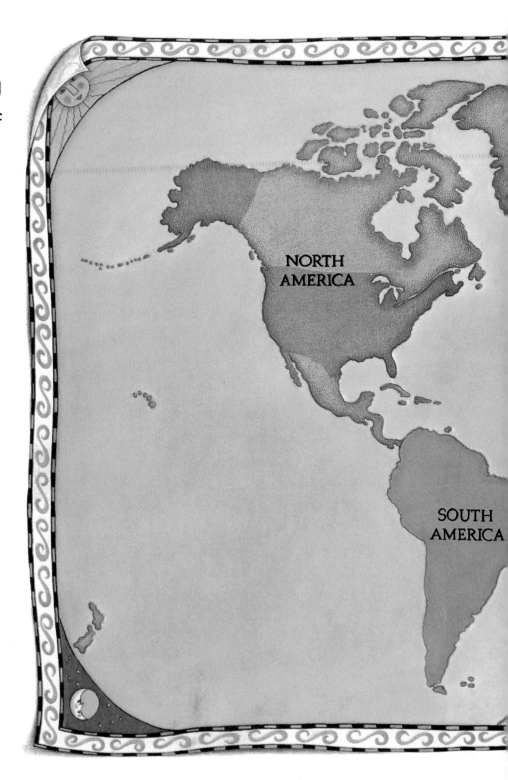

NORTH AMERICA

SOUTH AMERICA

OUR WORLD

EUROPE

ASIA

AFRICA

AUSTRALIA

ANTARCTICA

So here's how I find my special place on the map. First I look at the map of the world and find my country.

Then I look at the map of my country
and find my state.
Then I look at the map of my state
and find my town.

Then I look at the map of my town
and find my street.

And on my street I find my house.

And in my house I find my room.

And in my room I find me!
Just think . . .

. . . in rooms, in houses, on streets, in towns, in countries all over the world, everybody has their own special place on the map.

Just like me.

Just like me on the map.

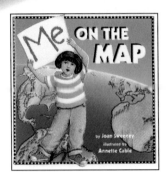

Think About the Story

1. How did the girl learn about her place in the world?

2. How do you think the girl feels about her special place on the map?

3. How would your map be different from the girl's map?

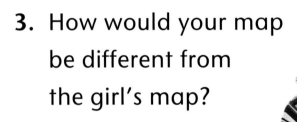

Complete a Web Word Find

Try finding some of the words from the story in a puzzle. Print out the puzzle from Education Place.

www.eduplace.com/kids

Make a Map

Draw a map of your neighborhood. Include streets, houses, and other buildings you see. Label each place on your map.

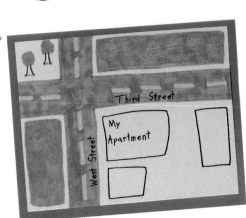

Write a Postcard

Write a postcard to a friend. Tell your friend about your special place on the map.

Dear Sam,
My special place is in Los Angeles.

Darren

Los Angeles California

Tips
- **Begin with a greeting.**
- **Write your name at the end.**

**Skill: How to
Read a Map**

- This map
  shows the
  world.

- It shows
  land and
  water.

- The labels
  tell the
  names of the
  continents,
  countries,
  and states.

Children of
the World

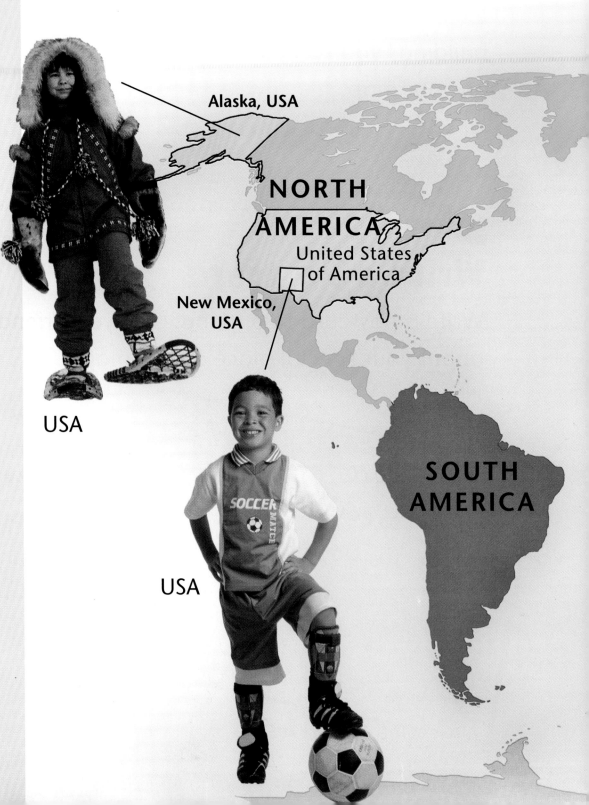

Alaska, USA

**NORTH
AMERICA**
United States
of America

New Mexico,
USA

USA

USA

**SOUTH
AMERICA**

Children all over the world live in
many different kinds of homes.
Take a look and see where they live!

ASIA

EUROPE

CHINA

China

IVORY COAST

AFRICA

AUSTRALIA

Ivory Coast

ANTARCTICA

This girl lives in Alaska.

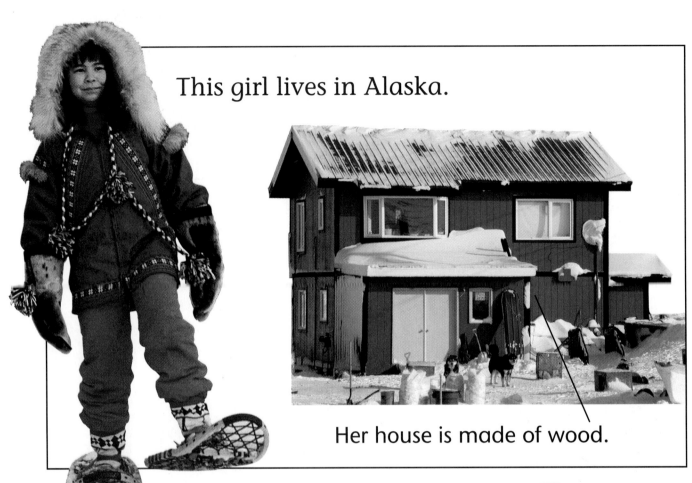

Her house is made of wood.

This boy lives in New Mexico.

His house is made of adobe.

This boy lives in China.

His house has a grass roof.

This girl
lives in the
Ivory Coast.

She lives in a tall apartment building.

Flying a Kite

Next you will read a story about a mother who makes a kite for her children. When the kite gets lost, the children find a surprise.

Words to Know

give	like
good	she'll
her	can't
little	isn't
try	doesn't
was	didn't
fly	it's
our	we've
kite	

Practice Sentences

1. When Mom was little, she had a kite.
2. She didn't know how to fly it.
3. Her father helped her.
4. We have a kite like Mom's.
5. Isn't that nice?
6. She'll try to get our kite up.
7. If we give it a good push, the kite will fly.
8. It's stuck in a tree and can't come down.
9. We've got to make a new kite.
10. Doesn't it look good?

87

The Kite

Alma Flor Ada

Illustrations by Vivi Escrivá

Santillana

The good news is . . .
Mama says she'll make us a kite like the ones
her father made when she was little.

The bad news is . . .
Mama doesn't know
how to make a kite.

The good news is . . .
Mama can learn.

The bad news is . . .
A kite isn't easy to make.

The good news is . . .
Mama didn't give up.
What a beautiful kite!

The bad news is . . .
It's raining, so we can't fly our kite.

The good news is . . .
The weather is perfect.
At last, we can fly our kite.

The bad news is . . .
The string broke and
the kite got away.

The good news is . . .
Mama says we can try to find it.

The bad news is . . .
We can't find it anywhere.

The good news is . . .
We've found a homeless cat.

The bad news is . . .
Mama says we can't take
the cat home with us.

The good news is . . .
We convinced her.

Meet the Author

Alma Flor Ada learned to read from her grandmother. When she was nine she knew she would be a writer. Now Alma Flor Ada writes books in Spanish and English. She says that the more you read, the better you will write.

Meet the Illustrator

Vivi Escrivá likes drawing pictures of children having fun. When she was little, she won first prize in an art contest. Later Vivi Escrivá worked for a TV show in Spain.

Learn more about Alma Flor Ada and Vivi Escrivá at Education Place.

www.eduplace.com/kids

Responding

Think About the Story

1. How does the mother learn how to make a kite?

2. What do the children learn from their mother?

3. How would it feel if you lost your kite?

Internet

Take an Online Poll

What is your favorite toy? Visit Education Place and take an online poll.

www.eduplace.com/kids

Weather Picture Dictionary

1. Think about the kinds of weather in the story.
2. Draw and label each kind.
3. Add other kinds of weather you know about.

Explaining

Write Sentences

What do you think happened to the kite in the story? Write some sentences to tell about where the kite might be.

 Tips

- **Make a list of some places the kite could be.**
- **Make sure each sentence has a naming word and an action word.**

105

Skill: How to Read Directions

- **Read** the list of materials.

- **Pictures** can give you extra information.

- **Complete** the steps in order.

- **Reread** any part that is unclear.

How to Make a Kite

Materials

- scrap paper

- kite paper (five inches by six inches)

- scissors

- two sticks, five inches and six inches long

- thread

- six feet of ribbon

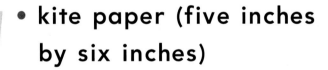

1 Fold your scrap paper in two. Draw a shape, cut it out, and open it up.

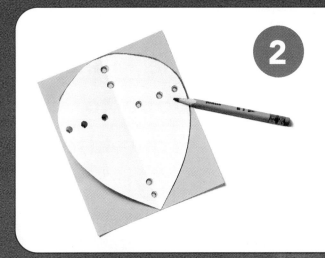

2 Trace your shape onto the kite paper and cut it out. Then make ten holes in your kite.

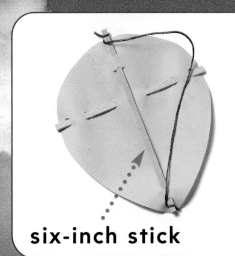

six-inch stick

3 Lace the two sticks in and out of the holes. Cut ten inches of thread and tie it to the six-inch stick.

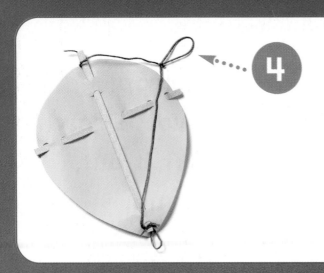

4 Make a loop of thread and tie it to the first thread.

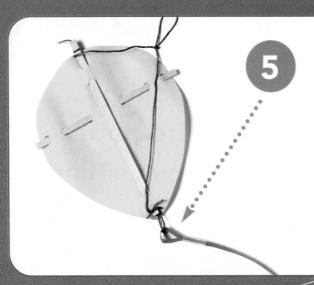

5 Tie a new loop to the bottom of the kite. Tie your ribbon to this loop. Your kite is all set to fly!

 Phonics

When you take some tests, your teacher will say a word. You need to find a word that has the same sound and fill in the circle to show the correct answer.

Tips

- Find the number.

- Listen to the teacher say a word.

- Read all the words.

- Fill in the whole circle.

1	have	thin	shake	bed
	○	○	●	○

Now see how one student figured
out the right answer.

How do I choose
the right answer?
First, I listen to
the teacher.

Then I read all the
words to see which
one has the same
sound as the word I
heard. *Shake* has
the same sound.

I fill in the
circle under
shake.

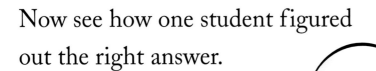

Read Together

Poetry

What is poetry?

- Poetry is a kind of writing that describes things in an interesting way.

- Some poems have rhyming words and some don't.

- Some poems have more than one part, or stanza.

Contents

Turtle, turtle

Turtle, turtle,
I wonder why
Other animals
Pass you by?

Turtles travel
Very slow,
Still I get
Where I want to go.

by Langston Hughes

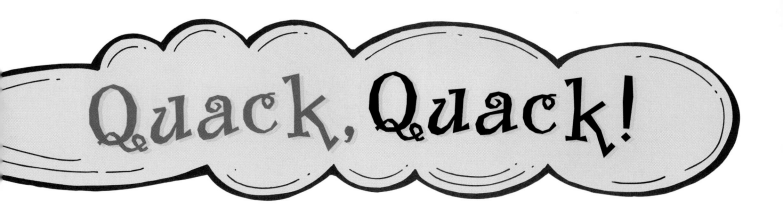

Quack, Quack!

We have two ducks. One blue. One black.
And when our blue duck goes "Quack-quack"
our black duck quickly quack-quacks back.
The quacks Blue quacks make her quite a quacker
but Black is a quicker quacker-backer.

by Dr. Seuss

Morning Sun

warming up
my bed
in the morning

the Sun
calls me
through the window

"wake up
get up
come on out"

by Francisco X. Alarcón

Sol matutino

calentando
mi cama
en la mañana

el Sol
me llama
por la ventana

"despierta
levántate
ven afuera"

por Francisco X. Alarcón

The Chipmunk

Chitter-chatter, chitter-chatter
is the chipmunk's steady patter,
even when he's eating acorns
(which he hopes will make him fatter).

by Jack Prelutsky

A little egg
in a nest of hay.
cheep-cheep.
crack-crack.
a little chick
pecked his shell away
cheep-cheep.
crack-crack.

by Tina Anthony
Age 7
England

A discovery!
On my frog's smooth green belly
there sits no button.

Haiku, Yayû

Write a Poem

You can write your own poem. Here's how to do it:

1. Choose a subject that you want to write about.

2. Decide if your poem will have rhyming words.

3. Think of some interesting ways to describe your subject.

When you finish, share your poem with others. Make a class poetry book by putting all your poems together.

Other Poetry Collections to Read

Soap Soup and Other Verses

by Karla Kuskin (HarperTrophy)

Everyday things take on a different look in this poetry book.

One, Two, Skip a Few!

illustrated by Roberta Arenson (Barefoot Books)

Here's a collection of poems about numbers.

Sports! Sports! Sports!
A Poetry Collection

selected by Lee Bennett Hopkins (HarperCollins)

Sports poems for everyone can be found in this book.

Animal Adventures

Two Feet, Four Feet

I have only two small feet,
But horses, dogs, and cows
    Have four.
I can walk and run with
    Mine.
So why do <u>they</u> need any
    More?

by Ilo Orleans

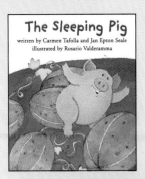

The Sleeping Pig
written by Carmen Tafolla and Jan Epton Seale
illustrated by Rosario Valderamma

How to Wake a Pig

In the next story, you'll read about a pig who won't get out of a watermelon patch. A small hero finally gets the pig to move.

Words to Know

morning	woke
found	nose
shout	whole
by	huge
out	use
show	tune
climb	went
go	lift
home	

Practice Sentences

1. If you went by your bed one morning and found a huge pig, would you lift it out?
2. You could walk by and shout, "Go home!"
3. Then climb up and tap the pig's small nose.
4. Sing a tune.
5. You could use the whole day to wake the pig.
6. Once you woke the pig, you could show it how to get home.

Meet the Authors

Carmen Tafolla

Jan Epton Seale

The authors first wrote this story in Spanish. Carmen Tafolla and Jan Epton Seale both live in Texas. Jan Epton Seale lives near Mexico. Carmen Tafolla has a daughter named Mari.

You can learn more about Carmen Tafolla and Jan Epton Seale at Education Place.

www.eduplace.com/kids

The Sleeping Pig

written by Carmen Tafolla and Jan Epton Seale

illustrated by Rosario Valderrama

Strategy Focus

Read Together

As you read, stop and think about what each animal does to wake Mrs. Pig.

One morning, Celina found a huge pig sleeping in the watermelon patch.

Celina began to shout. "Go home, Mrs. Pig! I wish you would go. You can't rest here in the watermelon patch. I can't pick my watermelons."

But huge Mrs. Pig didn't wake up.

137

A coyote came by and said, "Let me show you how to get Mrs. Pig out of the patch." The coyote began to howl and howl.

But huge Mrs. Pig did not wake up.

139

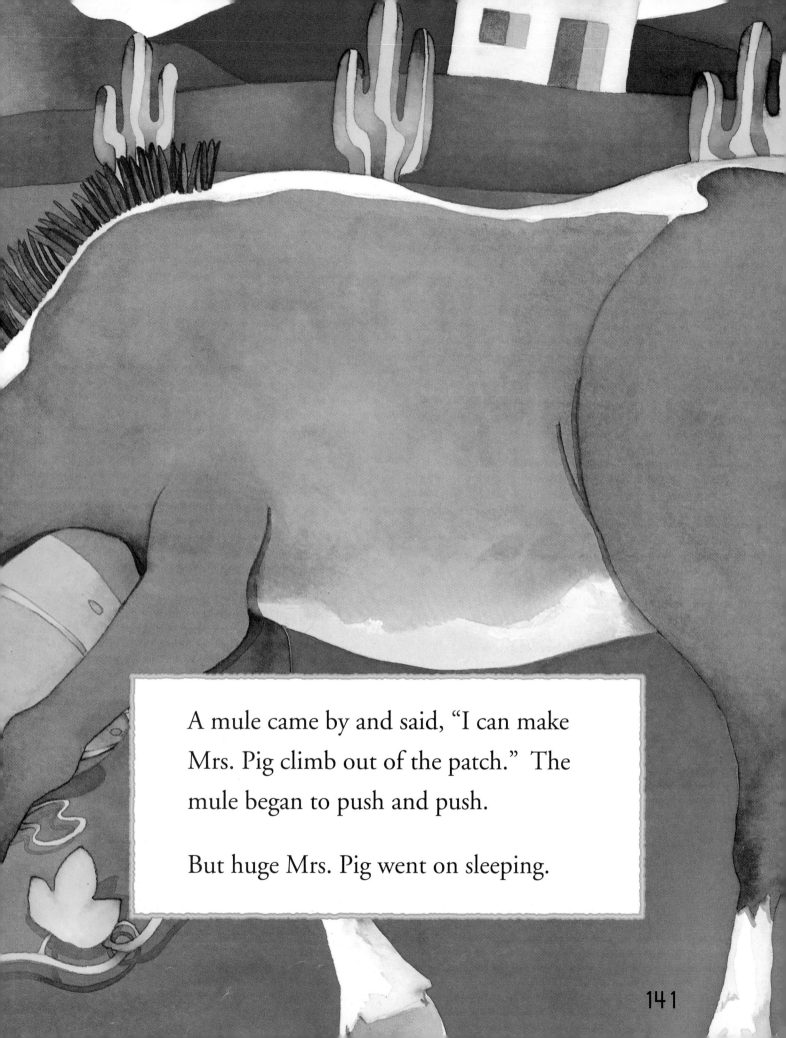

A mule came by and said, "I can make Mrs. Pig climb out of the patch." The mule began to push and push.

But huge Mrs. Pig went on sleeping.

A rabbit came by and said, "I will get Mrs. Pig out of the patch for you." The rabbit began to hop and hop.

But huge Mrs. Pig went on sleeping.

A snake came by and said, "I will use my tail to lift Mrs. Pig out of the patch." The snake began to pull and pull.

But huge Mrs. Pig wouldn't wake up.

144

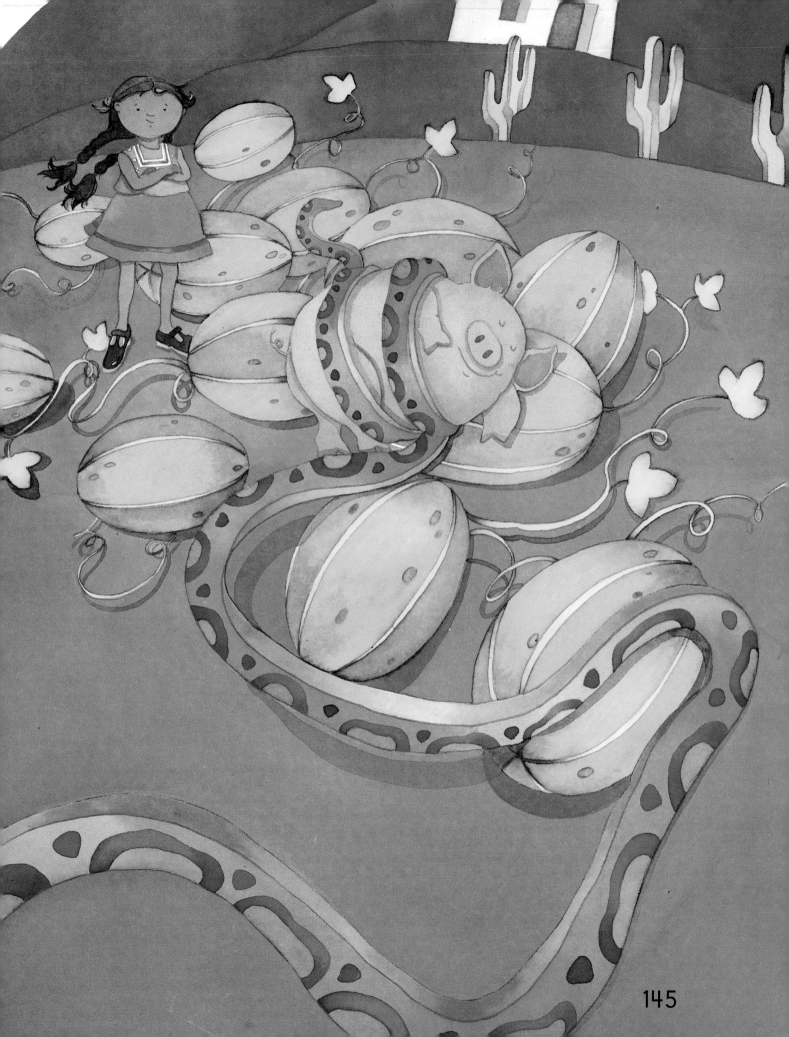

Then a cricket came by and said, "I know I am small and Mrs. Pig is huge. But just look at what I can do."

The cricket began to sing a tune.
Chirrr-chirrr-chirrr! Di-di-di-di!

149

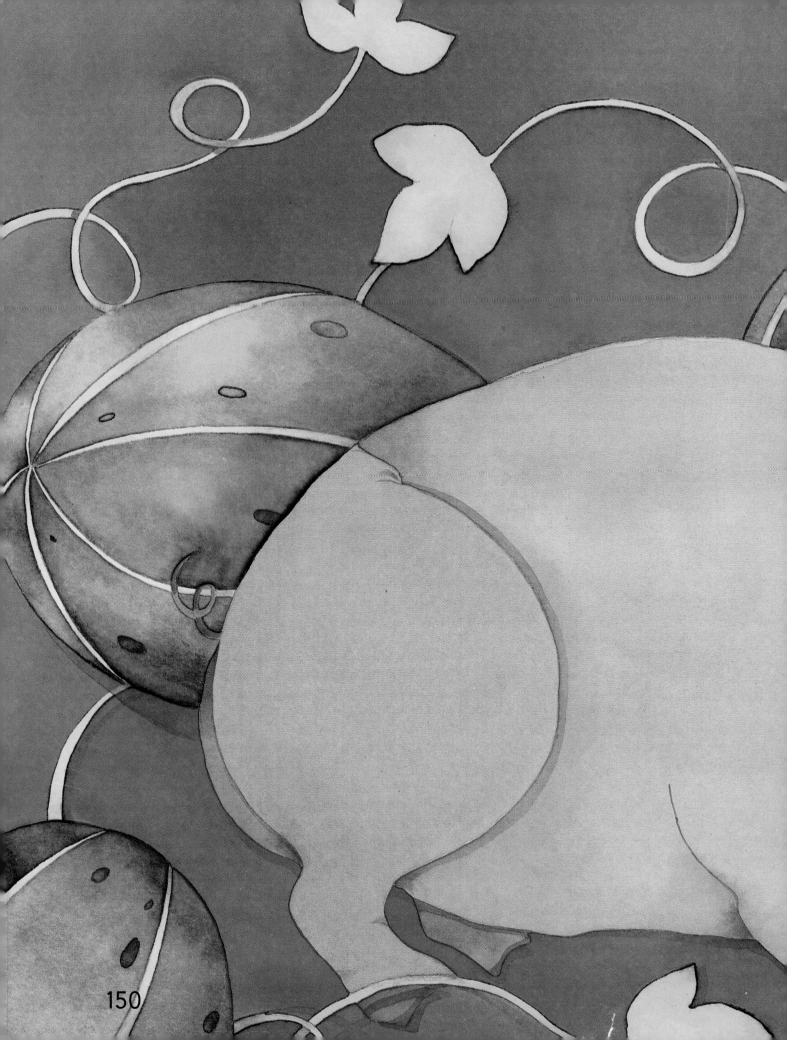

Mrs. Pig woke up fast. "Yes, it's time
to go home," she said with her nose up.
"A watermelon patch does not make a
good bed." And she left, sulking.

Celina thanked the small cricket. Then
they ate a whole watermelon to celebrate!

Read
Together

Meet the Illustrator
Rosario Valderrama

Rosario Valderrama was born in
Mexico City. When she draws, she tries
to remember the things she loved as a
child. She says young artists should try
to show their worlds to others.

 Internet

To find out more about Rosario Valderrama, visit
Education Place. **www.eduplace.com/kids**

The Sleeping Pig
written by Carmen Tafolla and Jan Epton Seale
illustrated by Rosario Valderamma

Think About the Story

1. How did Celina feel when she saw Mrs. Pig?

2. Why was the cricket the only animal who could wake Mrs. Pig?

3. What would you do if you were Celina?

Internet

Print Out Puppets

Print out story character puppets from Education Place to retell the story.

www.eduplace.com/kids

Make an Award

Make an award for the hero in the
story. Write a title for your award.

Best
Hero

Explaining

Write a Poster

How would you wake
a sleeping pig? Draw a
poster and write one sentence.
Share your poster with the class.

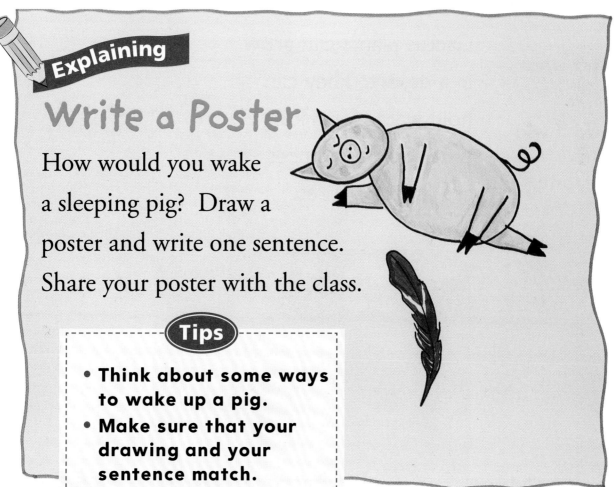

Tips

- **Think about some ways
  to wake up a pig.**
- **Make sure that your
  drawing and your
  sentence match.**

Skill: How to Read a Social Studies Article

- **Look** at the title and pictures.

- **Think** about what you know.

- **Predict** what you will learn.

- **Reread** if you do not understand.

What Is a Desert?

A desert is a dry place that gets little or no rain. There are many deserts all over the world.

Cactus plants can grow in a desert. They can hold water for a long time. Some cactuses are as big as trees.

Arizona, USA

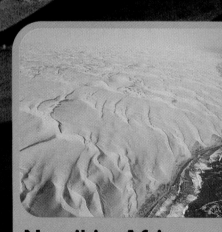
Namibia, Africa

Flowering Agave

Saguaro cactus

Claret Cup cactus

Birds, mice, snakes, and lizards are some of the animals that live in the desert.

The scorpion also makes its home in the desert.

Ostrich

Flap-Necked Chameleon

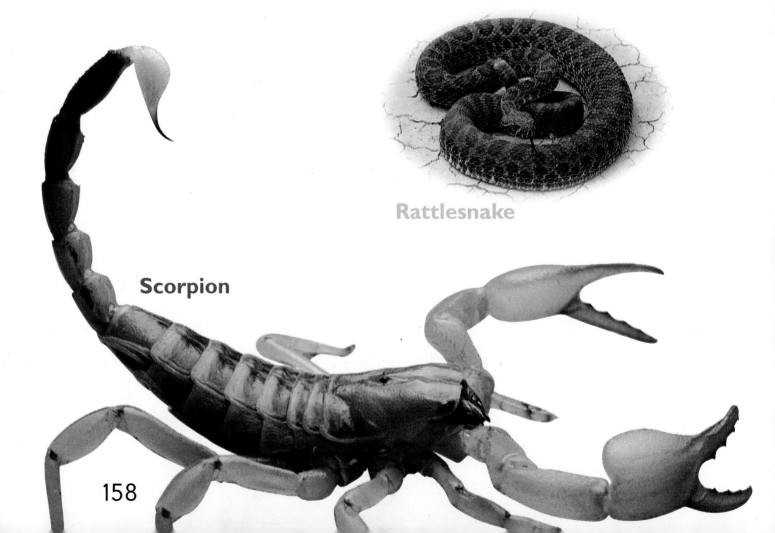

Rattlesnake

Scorpion

158

Some people move through the desert on camels. Camels can go days without food or water.

Would you like to see a desert?

A Description

A description is a picture in words that helps the reader to see, hear, taste, feel, and smell what you're writing about. Use this student writing as a model when you write your own description.

> A good **beginning** tells what the description is about.

> A good description includes **sense** words.

Fishing with My Dad

I have a big fishing rod with a small hook at the end. When I go fishing with my Dad, this is what I use. My Dad's fishing rod is tall and yellow with a big hook at the end.

160

He usually catches huge gray catfish.
I usually catch small minnows.

Meet the Author

Megan S.
Grade: one
State: Delaware
Hobbies: fishing, reading,
and writing
**What she'd like to be when
she grows up:** a teacher

**EEK!
There's a
Mouse in
the House**

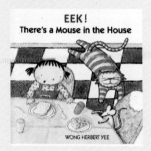

Animals in the House

In the next story, you'll read about some animals that mess up a little girl's house! How can she get rid of them?

Words to Know

cow	wall
table	me
now	he
door	EEK
there	sheep
through	eating
horse	

Practice Sentences

1. A cow, a sheep, and a horse came to a house.
2. "Now what could be in there?" asked the horse.
3. He went through the door.
4. The others went through, too.
5. By the wall was a table of things to eat.
6. A mouse was eating on the table.
7. "EEK!" said the cow and the sheep.
8. "The mouse can't hurt me," said the horse.

EEK!
There's a Mouse in the House

WONG HERBERT YEE

Read Together As you read the story, ask yourself about each animal and what it does.

EEK!

There's a mouse in the house.

Send in the cat
to chase that rat!

Uh-oh!

The cat knocked over a lamp.

Send in the dog
to catch that scamp!

Dear me!

The dog has broken a dish.

And now the cat is after the fish.

Send in the hog
to shoo that dog!

Oh my!

The hog is eating the cake.

Sending the hog
was a big mistake.

Send in the cow.

Send that cow NOW!

Oh no!

The cow is dancing with a mop.

Send in the sheep to make her stop!

Goodness!

The sheep is tangled
in yarn.

Send in the hen
from the barn!

Mercy!

The hen is laying eggs
on the table.

Send in the horse
from the stable!

Heavens!

The horse kicked a hole
in the wall.

Send in the elephant
to get rid of them ALL!

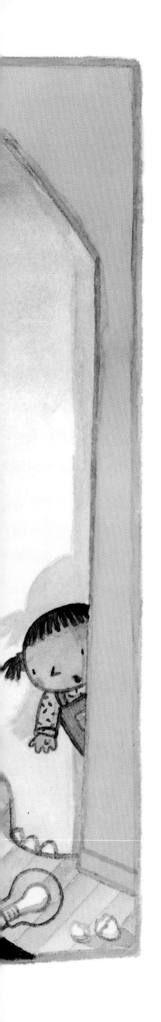

The elephant was BIG,
but he squeezed through the door.

Once he was in,
there was room for no more.

Out of the house marched
the cat and the cow.

Out came the horse and
the hen and the hog.

Out walked the sheep.

Out ran the dog.

But then from within,
there came a shout:

EEK! There's a mouse in the house!

182

Meet the Author and Illustrator

This is **Wong Herbert Yee**'s first children's book. While he was writing it, he read it to his young daughter, Ellen. If she laughed at a sentence, he kept it in the story.

Internet

Find out more about Wong Herbert Yee at Education Place.

www.eduplace.com/kids

183

Responding

EEK!
There's a Mouse in the House

WONG HERBERT YEE

Think About the Story

1. How did the girl feel about the mouse?

2. Was it a good idea for the girl to call in the animals? Why?

3. What would you do if you were the girl in this story?

Internet

Take an Online Poll

What animal from *EEK! There's a Mouse in the House* would you want for a pet? Visit Education Place to place your vote.

www.eduplace.com/kids

Act Out the Story

Act out the story with some partners. Each of you can be a different character. Make sure to use each character's actions.

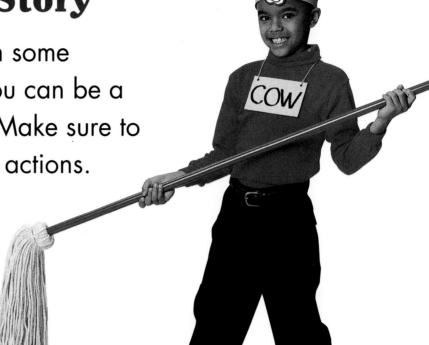

Write a List

Pick an animal from the story. Make a list of clean-up chores for the animal.

Tips

- **Think about what the animal needs to clean up.**
- **Number each thing on your list.**

Cat
1. Pick up the lamp.

Skill: How to Read a Pictograph

- A pictograph is a chart that uses pictures to compare things.

- These pictographs show the size of animals compared to people.

Animals Big and Small

Animals come in many shapes and sizes. Let's look at some of the biggest and smallest animals in the world.

Blue Whale

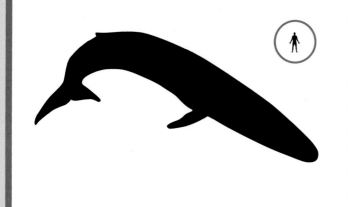

The biggest animal in the world is the blue whale. It can grow to 100 feet long. That's longer than sixteen six-foot men lying head to toe!

Giraffes are the tallest animals in the world.

Some giraffes grow as tall as nineteen feet.

That's taller than three men standing on top of each other's shoulders!

Harvest Mouse

Some harvest mice are no more than three inches long. That's about as long as a grown-up's finger!

Bee Hummingbird

The bee hummingbird from Cuba is just two inches long. That's shorter than a grown-up's thumb!

RED-EYED TREE FROG

BY JOY COWLEY · PHOTOGRAPHS BY NIC BISHOP

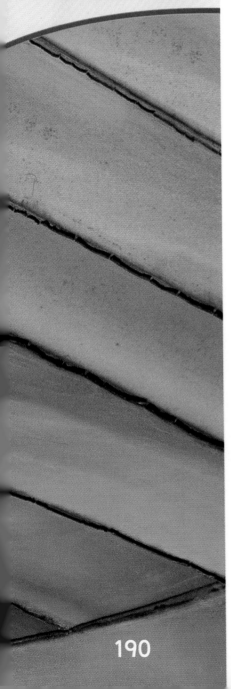

A Visit to the Rain Forest

You will read about a day in the life of a red-eyed tree frog in the next story.

Words to Know

been	evening
far	near
forest	rain
goes	wait
hungry	day
soon	away

Practice Sentences

1. My mom has been to the rain forest.

2. It's far away from where we live.

3. I will go the next time Mom goes.

4. We will hike all day.

5. When we are hungry, we will stop and eat.

6. We will spend the evening in a tent.

7. We will sit near a tree and wait for a red-eyed tree frog.

8. I hope we go soon!

RED-EYED TREE FROG

BY JOY COWLEY · PHOTOGRAPHS BY NIC BISHOP

Strategy Focus

Read Together What do you think the red-eyed tree frog will do? Read the story to find out.

Evening comes to the rain forest.

The macaw
and the toucan
will soon go to sleep.

But the red-eyed tree frog has
been asleep all day.

It wakes up hungry.
What will it eat?

Here is an iguana.
Frogs do not eat iguanas.

Do iguanas eat frogs?
The red-eyed tree frog does
not wait to find out.
It hops onto another branch.

The frog is hungry but it will
not eat the ant.

It will not eat the katydid.

Will it eat the caterpillar?
No!

The caterpillar is poisonous.

Something moves near the frog.
Something slips and slithers along a branch.
It is a hungry boa snake.

The snake flicks its tongue.
It tastes frog in the air.
Look out, frog!

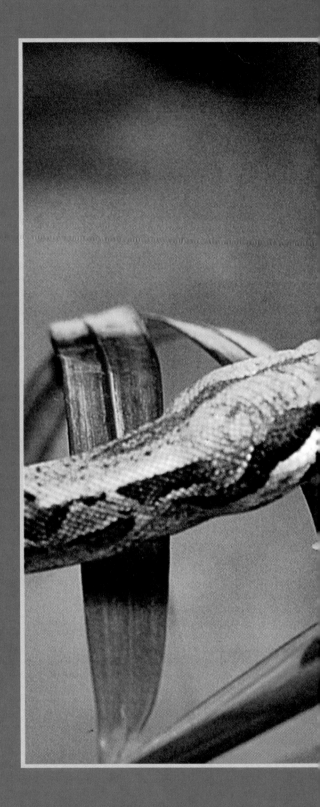

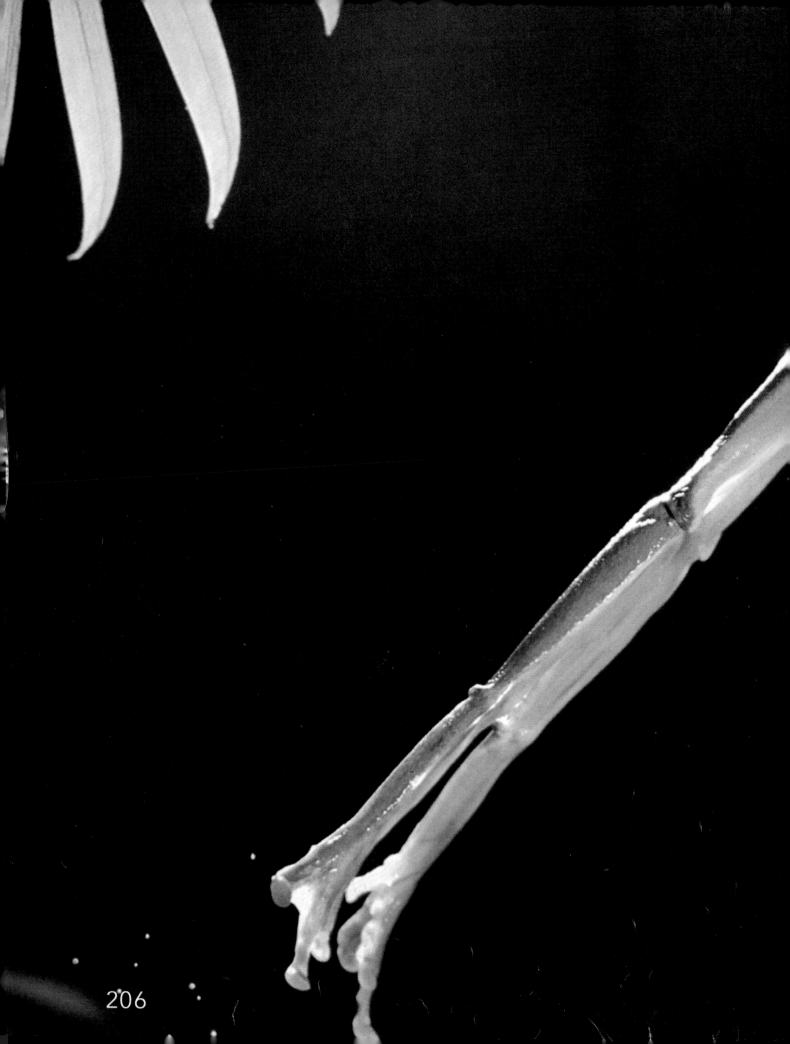

JUMP!

JUMP!

The frog lands on a leaf,
far away from the boa.
What does the frog see on
the leaf?

A moth!

Crunch, crunch, crunch!

The tree frog is no longer hungry.
It climbs onto a leaf.

The red-eyed tree frog shuts its eyes . . .

and goes to sleep . . .

as morning comes to the rain forest.

Meet the Author and the Photographer

Joy Cowley loves animals, especially frogs. When she saw these pictures, she liked them very much. She decided to write a children's book to go with them.

Nic Bishop went to the rain forest to take photographs of the red-eyed tree frogs. One frog became a family pet.

Visit Education Place to learn more about Joy Cowley and Nic Bishop.

www.eduplace.com/kids

215

Responding

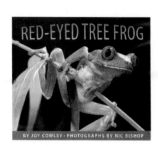

Think About the Story

1. Do you think this rain forest is quiet or noisy? Why?

2. What do you think the red-eyed tree frog has learned about living in the rain forest?

3. Would you like to visit the rain forest? Why?

Go on a Web Field Trip

Visit a rain forest at Education Place.

www.eduplace.com/kids

Comparing Sizes

A red-eyed tree frog is nearly as long as this ruler. Find things in your classroom that are about the same size.

Creating

Write a Riddle

Write a riddle about one of the animals in the story. Have a partner read your riddle and guess the animal.

Tips

- Study a picture of the animal.
- Use describing words.

Who has a yellow stripe and many legs?

Skill: How to Read a Poem

- **Read** the title to see what the poem is about.

- **Read** the poem.

- **Listen** for any rhyming words.

The Snake

Don't ever make
the bad mistake
of stepping on
the sleeping snake

because

his jaws

might be awake.

by Jack Prelutsky

Snake, 20th century,
Niki de Saint-Phalle, b. 1930, French
painted polyester

218

THE TOUCAN

Of all the birds I know, few can
Boast of as large a bill as the toucan.
Yet I can think of one who can,
And if you think a while, too, you can:
Another toucan
In the zoo can.

by Pyke Johnson, Jr.

Toucan Design on Mola, San Blas Archipelago, Panama

✓ Filling in the Blank

In some tests you must decide which answer choice best fills in the blank. How do you choose the best answer? Look at this sample test for *Red-Eyed Tree Frog*. The correct answer is shown.

Tips

- Read the directions carefully. Make sure you know how to mark your answers.

- Try out each word in the sentence. Ask yourself: Which word fits best?

- Fill in the whole circle.

- Look back at the story if you need to.

> **Read the sentence. Fill in the circle next to the best answer.**
>
> 1 The red-eyed tree frog _____ all day.
>
>   ● sleeps
>   ○ climbs
>   ○ eats

Now see how one student figured out
the best answer.

First, I read the
directions. Next, I
read the sentence to
myself using each
answer choice.

I am looking for the
answer that tells
what the frog does
all day. I look back
in the story. It says
that the red-eyed
tree frog sleeps all
day.

The last two
answers do not tell
about the frog in
the daytime. Now I
see why the first
word best
completes the
sentence.

Glossary

A

anywhere
Anywhere means in any place. You can sit anywhere you like.

B

ball
A **ball** is something that is round. Miguel hit the **ball** with the bat.

barn
A **barn** is a kind of building on a farm. A farmer keeps his cows and pigs in the **barn**.

beautiful
Beautiful means very nice to look at or hear. Anna drew a picture of a **beautiful** rainbow.

began
To **begin** means to start. School **began** in September.

boa

A **boa** is a kind of snake. A **boa** can live in the rain forest.

C

caterpillar

A **caterpillar** is an insect that looks like a worm. A **caterpillar** will change into a butterfly.

celebrate

To **celebrate** is to do something special for an event. We went to the park to **celebrate** my birthday.

convinced

To **convince** means to talk someone into something. I **convinced** my mother to let me go on the trip.

country

A **country** is a place where people live and share the same laws. There are many **countries** in the world.

coyote

A **coyote** is an animal that looks like a small wolf. The **coyote** didn't look much bigger than a dog.

cricket

A **cricket** is a small insect that looks like a grasshopper. Jamal saw the **cricket** jump.

D

dancing

To **dance** means to move your body to music. Jan and her friends like **dancing** at parties.

E

Earth

Earth is the planet we live on. **Earth** looks round when you see it from space.

easy

Easy means not hard to do. Riding my bike is **easy**.

elephant

An **elephant** is a very big animal with thick skin, big ears, and a long trunk. The **elephant** was the biggest animal in the circus.

eyes

Eyes are the parts of the body that let it see. The kitten closed its **eyes** and went to sleep.

F

fancy

Fancy means prettier or better than usual. We had a **fancy** cake at the party.

G

giant

Giant means much bigger than usual. Michael looked up at the **giant** tree.

H

heavy
Heavy means hard to lift. The box of toys was too **heavy** to carry.

hide
To **hide** something is to put it where nobody will see it. When I **hide**, my friends can't find me.

howl
To **howl** is to make a long cry like a dog, coyote, or wolf. My dog will **howl** when she's lonely.

I

iguana
An **iguana** is a kind of lizard. Tanya wanted an **iguana** for a pet.

inside
To be **inside** means to be in something. I'm staying **inside** the house because it's raining.

K

katydid

A **katydid** is a large green insect like a grasshopper. A **katydid** will rub its wings together to make a noise.

L

laying

To **lay** an egg is to make an egg. The hen was **laying** eggs in her nest.

M

macaw

A **macaw** is a large parrot.
The **macaw** has a strong, curved beak.

marched

To **march** with someone is to take the same size steps at the same time. The band **marched** in the big parade.

mercy

To say **Mercy** is to show surprise. **Mercy!** That was a close call.

mouse

A **mouse** is a very small animal with a long tail, short fur, and sharp teeth. The **mouse** likes to eat cheese.

moves

To **move** is to go from one place to another. A bird **moves** from tree to tree by flying.

N

news

News is a story about things that are happening. My mother watches the **news** on television.

P

perfect

If something is **perfect**, it is just right. It was a **perfect** day for flying our kite.

plain

Plain means very simple. I put my lunch in a **plain** brown paper bag.

poisonous

A **poison** is something that can cause sickness or death. A rattlesnake is a **poisonous** animal.

R

rabbit

A **rabbit** is an animal with long ears and soft fur. A **rabbit** can hop very fast.

raining

To **rain** means to fall as drops of water. Get your umbrella because it's **raining**.

rough

Something that is **rough** does not feel even. The bumpy road was very **rough**.

S

smooth

Something that is **smooth** feels even and has no rough spots. The ice at the rink was very **smooth**.

special
Special means important and not like all the rest. Holidays and birthdays are **special** days.

street
A **street** is a road in a city or town. Sue lives on a busy **street**.

T

tail
A **tail** is part of an animal's body. Laura's dog wags its **tail** when it gets a treat.

tangled
Tangle means to be all mixed up. The kite's string got **tangled** in the tree.

tongue
The **tongue** is a part of the body inside the mouth. Your **tongue** helps you eat and speak.

toucan

A **toucan** is a colorful bird with a very long, large bill. Amy was excited to see a **toucan** flying in the rain forest.

town

A **town** is a place where people live and work. My **town** is smaller than a city.

W

wait

To **wait** means to stay someplace until something happens. We **wait** at the corner until the school bus comes.

watermelon

A **watermelon** is a big sweet fruit that is pink or red inside. **Watermelon** is a good snack in the summer.

weather

Weather is what it is like outside. Jim goes swimming in warm **weather**.

Acknowledgments

For each of the selections listed below, grateful acknowledgment is made for permission to excerpt and/or reprint original or copyrighted material, as follows:

Selections

EEK! There's a Mouse in the House, by Wong Herbert Yee. Copyright © 1992 by Wong Herbert Yee. Reprinted by permission of Houghton Mifflin Company. All rights reserved.

The Kite, by Alma Flor Ada, illustrated by Vivi Escrivá. Copyright © 1999 by Santillana USA Publishing Co., Inc. Reprinted by permission of the publisher.

Me on the Map, by Joan Sweeney, illustrated by Annette Cable. Text copyright © 1996 by Joan Sweeney. Illustrations copyright © 1996 by Annette Cable. Reprinted by permission of Random House Children's Books, a division of Random House Inc.

Moving Day, by Robert Kalan, illustrated by Yossi Abolafia. Text copyright © 1996 by Robert Kalan. Illustrations copyright © 1996 by Yossi Abolafia. Reprinted by permission of HarperCollins Publishers.

Red-Eyed Tree Frog, by Joy Cowley, photographs by Nic Bishop. Published by Scholastic Press, a division of Scholastic, Inc. Text copyright © 1999 by Joy Cowley. Photographs copyright © 1999 by Nic Bishop. Reprinted by permission of Scholastic, Inc.

Poetry

"A discovery!" by Yayû from *Birds, Frogs and Moonlight,* translated by Sylvia Cassedy and Kunihiro Suetake. Copyright © 1967 by Doubleday and Co. Reprinted by permission of Ellen Cassedy.

"A little egg," by Tina Anthony from *Miracles: Poems by Children of the English Speaking World,* edited by Richard Lewis. Copyright © 1966 by Richard Lewis. Reprinted by permission of Richard Lewis.

"The Chipmunk" from *Zoo Doings,* by Jack Prelutsky. Copyright © 1983 by Jack Prelutsky. Reprinted by permission of HarperCollins Publishers.

"Morning Sun/ Sol matutino" from *Laughing Tomatoes and Other Spring Poems/Jitomates Risueños y Otros Poemas de Primavera,* by Francisco X. Alarcón. Copyright © 1997 by Francisco Alarcón. Reprinted by permission of the publisher, Children's Book Press, San Francisco, CA.

"Quack, Quack!" from *Oh Say Can You Say?,* by Dr. Seuss. TM & copyright © by Dr. Seuss Enterprises, L.P., 1979. Reprinted by permission of Random House Children's Books, a division of Random House, Inc.

"The Snake" from *Zoo Doings,* by Jack Prelutsky. Copyright © 1983 by Jack Prelutsky. Reprinted by permission of HarperCollins Publishers.

"The Toucan," from *Pyke's Poems,* by Pyke Johnson, Jr., published by Shorelands Publishing Company, 1992. Copyright © by Pyke Johnson, Jr. Reprinted by permission of the author.

"Turtle" from *The Sweet and Sour Animal Book,* by Langston Hughes. Copyright © 1994 (text) by Romana Bass & Arnold Rampersad, Administrators of the Estate of Langston Hughes. Reprinted by permission of Oxford University Press, Inc.

"Two Feet, Four Feet," by Ilo Orleans. Copyright © 1992 by Ilo Orleans. Reprinted by permission of Karen S. Solomon.

Special thanks to the following teachers whose students' compositions appear as Student Writing Models: Cheryl Claxton, Florida; Patricia Kopay, Delaware; Susana Llanes, Michigan; Joan Rubens, Delaware; Nancy Schulten, Kentucky; Linda Wallis, California

Credits

Photography

3 (t) © Joan Steiner. **7** Lance Nelson/The Stock Market. **8** (t) image Copyright © 2000 PhotoDisc, Inc. **10** (t) CORBIS/David A. Northcott. **12** (bkgd) image Copyright © 2000 PhotoDisc, Inc. (icon) © Joan Steiner. **12–13** © Joan Steiner. **43** (t) Courtesy William Morrow. **44** (l) image Copyright © 2000 PhotoDisc, Inc. (r) Artville. **46** (t) CORBIS/Stuart Westmorland. (b) J.H. (Pete) Carmichael. **47** (t) Dave King/Dorling Kindersley. (b) J.H. (Pete) Carmichael. **48** NHPA/Anthony Bannister. **49** CORBIS/Annie Griffiths Belt. **54** (t) John Zich/Mercury Pictures. (b) Courtesy Annette Cable. **82** (t) Chris Arend/Alaska Stock Images. (b) Rubberball Productions. **83** (t) Jian Chen/Stock Connection/PictureQuest. (b) Michael Dwyer/Stock Boston/PictureQuest. **84** (tl) Chris Arend/Alaska Stock Images. (tr) CORBIS/Galen Rowell. (bl) Garry Adams/IndexStock. (br) Rubberball Productions. **85** (tl) CORBIS/The Purcell Team. (tr) Jian Chen/Stock Connection/PictureQuest. (bl) Michael Dwyer/Stock Boston/PictureQuest. (br) Christopher Morris/Black Star/PictureQuest. **102** Courtesy Alma Flor Ada. **103** Courtesy Vivi Escrivá. **106–9** (bkgd) image Copyright © 2000 PhotoDisc, Inc. **108** Lynda Richardson. **109** (t) Lawrence Migdale/Stock Boston. (b) Lynda Richardson. **112–3** Lance Nelson/The Stock Market. **114–5** image Copyright © 2000 PhotoDisc, Inc. **116** Tim Davis/Tony Stone Images.

117 Paul Chauncey/The Stock Market. **118** Laurie Rubin/The Image Bank. **120** Daniel J. Cox/Tony Stone Images. **122–3** Tim Davis/Photo Researchers, Inc. **124–5** Frank Moscati/The Stock Market. **126** John Lei/Stock Boston. **128** (icon) image Copyright © 2000 PhotoDisc, Inc. **132** (l) Courtesy Carmen Tafolla. (r) Paul Buck/Mercury Pictures. **153** Courtesy Rosario Valderrama. **156–7** © Jim Brandenburg/Minden Pictures. **156** (bl) © Carr Clifton/Minden Pictures. (br) © Jim Brandenburg/Minden Pictures. **157** (bl) Frans Lanting/Minden Pictures. (bm) Brian Stablyk/Tony Stone Images. (br) Kerrick James/Tony Stone Images. **158** (t) (m) (bl) Frans Lanting/Minden Pictures. (br) © Jim Brandenburg/Minden Pictures. **159** Will & Deni McIntyre/Tony Stone Images. **160** image Copyright © 2000 PhotoDisc, Inc. **183** Courtesy Wong Herbert Yee. **186–7** Mike Johnson Marine Natural History Photography. **188** Corbis Royalty Free. **189** (t) CORBIS/George McCarthy. (b) Robert Tyrrell Photography. **190** © Nic Bishop Photography. **192** (bkgd) DigitalVision/Picture Quest. **215** (tl) © Terry Coles. (tr) Michael P.L. Fogden/Bruce Coleman/PictureQuest. (bl) David Aubrey/The Stock Market. (br) Courtesy Nic Bishop. **216** image Copyright © 2000 PhotoDisc, Inc. **217** CORBIS/David A. Northcott. **218** Snake, 20th century. Niki de Saint-Phalle, b. 1930, French. painted polyester. 59 in height. Private Collection. Christie's Images, Inc. **219** CORBIS/Kevin Schafer. **222** images Copyright © 2000 PhotoDisc, Inc. **223** Kim Taylor/Dorling Kindersley. **224** images Copyright © 2000 PhotoDisc, Inc. **225** image Copyright © 2000 PhotoDisc, Inc. **226** PhotoSpin. **227** (t) Artville. (b) image Copyright © 2000 PhotoDisc, Inc. **228** image Copyright © 2000 PhotoDisc, Inc. **229** image Copyright © 2000 PhotoDisc, Inc. **231** (t) ©Frans Lanting/Minden Pictures. (b) Artville.

Assignment Photography

15, 45 (t), **53, 80. 105, 128–9** Joel Benjamin. **131, 163, 184** Michelle Joyce. **155, 185** Allan Landau. **111, 221** Tony Scarpetta.

Illustration

12–13, 87 Toby Williams. **115–126** (borders) Eileen Hine. **130, 132, 133–154** Rosario Valderrama. **163, 184** Sherri Haab. **191** Mircea Catusanu. **217** Lizi Boyd.